W9-BYZ-514

Forced to Retire

pg 36

Joel M. Johnson, CFP®

Copyright © 2014 by Joel M. Johnson

All rights reserved. No part of this book may be used or reproduced in any manner whatsoever without written permission of the author.

Printed in The United States of America.

ISBN: 978-0692329399

Published by

Big Man Publishing

Contents

Regulatory Issues

Notes to Readers

This publication contains the opinions and ideas of its author. The strategies outlined in this book may not be suitable for every individual and are not guaranteed or warranted to produce any particular results. Presentation of performance data herein does not imply that similar results will be achieved in the future. Any such data are provided merely for illustrative and discussion purposes; rather than focusing on the time periods used or the results derived. The reader should focus instead on the underlying principles.

This book is sold with the understanding that neither publisher nor author, through this book, is engaged in rendering legal, tax, investment, insurance, financial, accounting or other professional advice or services. If the reader requires such advice or services, a competent professional should be consulted. Relevant laws vary from state to state.

No warranty is made with respect to the accuracy or the completeness of the information contained herein, and both the author and the publisher specifically disclaim any responsibility for any liability, loss, or risk, personal or otherwise, that is incurred as a consequence, directly or indirectly, of the use and application of any of the contents of this book.

Lastly, this book is written under the right of the First Amendment to the Constitution of the United States. This book is written as an outside business activity from my investment advisory and securities business.

The ideas expressed are not meant to be taken as advice that you can act upon.

You should find an individual advisor that you trust to implement these ideas after determining if they are appropriate and suitable for your unique situation.

Insurance Products and Annuities are guaranteed by the insurance companies themselves. The safety of these accounts is dependent on the claims paying ability of the insurance companies.

Introduction

When you unexpectedly receive notice that your job is abruptly ending or learn that you are being offered a separation package, the decisions you need to make - for yourself and for your family - can create considerable anxiety and stress. That's perfectly understandable.

Some people even experience increased anxiety as a planned retirement approaches, often as long as five years in advance. That apprehension often continues for years after retirement, as the major changes that occur can be jarring, uncertain and upsetting.

The day that you retire represents a fundamental change in your life. Therefore, it should also trigger fundamental changes in the way you invest and spend your money. Your relationship with money changes, because you go from earning and growing your nest egg to preserving your nest egg and creating cash flow.

The purpose of this book is to simplify the many decisions that you need to make, provide you with a guide to evaluate your choices, and help you figure out what to do to build confidence in your future. We will provide ways to reduce your stress and help you regain your financial footing. And we'll suggest productive approaches to take immediate action to improve your situation and transition into your future, empowered.

There are seven crucial areas that will affect your financial well-being, and this book will tackle them, one at a time. Keep in mind that the older you are, the higher the cost of making mistakes in each of these areas. You have the most to gain - or lose - by the choices that you make.

The tension is heightened, and the impact more acute, when retirement is thrust upon you. But the decisions are no less critical, regardless of the time you have to make them.

One cautionary note at the outset. Turning to financial

gurus, the media, and major Wall Street stockbrokers – the conventional financial advice infrastructure - could be the worst place to get direction at a time of personal uncertainty, because of the potential conflicts of interest and stale ideas.

All progress starts with telling yourself the truth. The truth about how much you have, and where it is invested. The truth about who you love and what you care about. The truth about your fears. The truth about your legacy, and the impact that the choices you make now will have on that legacy.

Let's dig into the seven questions that you need to answer for yourself. By doing so, you will pave your way to a better retirement.

Chapter 1

Do I Need to Find Another Job?

There are two different ways to phrase this important question. How you ask the question will lead to very different answers – answers that will help guide your decision-making.

It boils down to two words – "need" and "want." One way to ask the question is, "Do I *need* to find another job?" The other way is to ask, "Do I *want* to find another job?" Let's deal with each separately.

First, "Do I *need* to find another job?"

To answer this question and have sufficient peace of

mind to move forward, you should have a retirement income plan. The plan would develop financial projections based on what you have already saved from other sources of income that will be available to you during retirement (such as Social Security or pensions, or perhaps a spouse still working).

For our clients, we create a retirement income plan or a retirement income analysis. It takes a snapshot of exactly where you are today and your objective for the level of income you want to have coming into the household during your retirement.

Obviously if you're retiring today, we need to create that income stream right away. You start with what you want - your immediate needs for money coming in. Then we say, "Okay, what do you have that can create a source of income at the level you need? Is it savings? Is it a brokerage account? Is it future pensions or Social Security?" In fact, there is a software program that will chart that information and plug those pieces in as they start to come into your life.

If you're retired at 58, for example, you're not going to

get Social Security until age 62, in most instances. Of course, you might decide to wait until age 66 or 70, but you're certainly not going to receive it before age 62. Therefore, you need a certain amount of income to bridge that gap.

A related question: if you're able to begin taking a pension, should you do so now or later? We'll deal with that subject in greater detail later in this book, but as you develop a retirement income plan to help you decide whether you can afford not to work or you need to find another job, that is an aspect you should consider.

Here's another big issue: do you have any debt? And do you have debt outside of your mortgage? One of the most powerful things that you can do – not only as a retiree, but as a human being, is to walk through life without owing anything to anybody. In my opinion, it is acceptable to have a mortgage. Other debts, however, from depreciating assets such as automobiles or vacations that you put on a credit card, need to be resolved as rapidly as possible. Is there a way to diminish, then eliminate, that debt without severely affecting your day-to-day life?

Next, we move to budgets. Do you feel that you need to have a budget in order to plan effectively? Or are you the type of person that merely wants to make certain there is some money coming in and that you have emergency money set aside? Although some people don't believe a budget is necessary, it can be quite helpful in order to determine, step-by-step and with confidence, what your retirement income needs are likely to be.

You must also consider this: Is there anyone who depends on you for financial support? If there is, and you have just learned that you will be retiring sooner than you had expected, it may not be possible to continue supporting them – at least not in the manner to which they have become accustomed. That may be a tough conversation to have, but it is essential to figuring out the level of income you require.

Answering the pivotal question, "Do I *need* to get another job?" fundamentally depends on two factors: 1) what assets do I have coming into my household, and 2) can I live on that particular income stream?

You need to develop as accurate a projection as possible of the income you can anticipate coming in for the rest of your life. If you don't feel comfortable developing the information and arriving at a conclusion yourself, you may need to turn to a financial professional. As mentioned earlier, you should do so with care.

Once those answers are in place, it will be evident whether fulltime employment is necessary, or a part-time job – especially doing something you really like – would be sufficient. In many cases, all that is needed is 15 or 20 hours a week, allowing you to pick up some extra cash flow which would allow you to forego tapping into your retirement nest egg.

Now, what about the other question, "Do I *want* to find another job?"

This is a very different question, but definitely one worth your attention – especially if you have determined that the answer to the question of *need* is "no." We have a great many clients in our financial services practice that work because they want to. Financial necessity is not driving their decision.

Often, these individuals elect to work because they want more fulfillment or purpose in their retirement. They do not want to play golf endlessly or tinker around the house every day. They might have a hobby that has been repressed or limited throughout their lives and now that they are retired from their primary profession, they can work part-time pursuing that hobby.

Here's an example: I have a client who is retired. He is a very, very handy person, so he sought out a part-time position at Home Depot. Home Depot loved the fact that he preferred part-time work, about 20 to 22 hours a week. They also appreciated – as you might imagine – that they don't have to pay healthcare or benefits, because he is all set with both. He loves the idea that he gets to be around building supplies, people asking for advice, and contractors who are building homes or doing renovations. It is a win-win. He can have interaction with people in ways that are very fulfilling to him, and he can earn an additional $200.00 to $400.00 per week. It is money that he doesn't need to meet his financial obligations, but he works nonetheless - because he derives other benefits.

There are times when we simply want to work, even if we have determined it is not financially essential. In other instances, our personal financial requirements make a new job absolutely necessary. Whether your retirement is planned or sudden, after careful consideration and analysis it is important for you to know whether you *need* to find another job or you *want* to find another job.

Chapter 2

Should I Collect Unemployment?

Even though they have been essentially forced into early retirement – often the result of a layoff or downsizing at the plant or company, many people I've worked through the years with have had a tremendous amount of guilt about collecting unemployment compensation. You shouldn't feel guilty. Not even for a minute.

It is important to understand that unemployment is a form of insurance. In a nutshell, here's how it operates. While you were working, your employer paid into the unemployment insurance system. Unemployment is basically a federal program that is administered by states. The state that your company operates in, or the state that you worked in, collected some money from your employer with every paycheck they issued. That money goes into a fund, and since every company doesn't lay everybody off at the same time, the few cents that are collected on every dollar of payroll accumulate and the fund grows. When layoffs occurs, the state's unemployment insurance fund pays out benefits to the individuals who have been laid off.

Therefore, you should not feel guilty. You are not taking money away from the government. You are not taking money away from taxpayers. That money has been set aside specifically to pay unemployment benefits. You paid into the system, you should certainly be able to get money out of the system when you are eligible. (Technically, you didn't pay in - your employer, as a cost of having you work there, paid in.) The point is this: don't be uncomfortable collecting unemployment.

There are a couple of questions that often come up regarding collecting unemployment. One is "Can I collect Social Security and unemployment at the same time?" The answer is yes. You can collect Social Security and, if you are eligible for unemployment, you can simultaneously collect unemployment.

It is advisable to notify both parties, the Social Security system and unemployment office (usually administered by the Department of Labor in your state), that you are collecting both benefits. That should not cause any problems, because Social Security specifically does not disqualify you from collecting unemployment benefits.

A pension is another matter. If you are collecting a pension, it may disqualify you from unemployment benefits. For example, let's say that I worked for AT&T for the past 20 years and they terminated my job. If I go to collect unemployment at the same time I file for my pension from that company, I could lose eligibility for my unemployment benefit by collecting the pension from that company. That is why sometimes it makes better sense to forego the pension until you exhaust your unemployment benefits.

Let's use that same basic scenario, but change it slightly. In this version, I was laid off by AT&T, but I have a previous pension from United Airlines. I can collect my

Forced to Retire

pension from United Airlines and file for unemployment benefits based on my work at AT&T. In this scenario, I will not be disqualified from the unemployment benefits because my United Airlines pension is from a different company than the most recent company that I worked for, and which issued the layoff.

Unemployment uses something called your "base year" - the last year that you worked. If the last company you worked for, which formed that base year for the calculation of your unemployment benefits, is not the company that you are collecting a pension from, you should not encounter any difficulty in receiving both unemployment and pension benefits. It is always safest, however, to check with your state Department of Labor, as well as the company from which you are to be receiving a pension.

Another question that occasionally arises is, "Can I collect unemployment while I'm getting severance?" This is decided on a case-by-case basis, determined by how the company codes your severance pay in its filing with the state. You might receive severance pay by receiving a check every pay period for six months after being terminated. Or you may receive a lump sum severance check. How the company codes your severance payment – and whether it is therefore considered as wages within the state system - will determine whether you will be able to collect unemployment right away or whether you will be required to wait.

Most important is that immediately upon separation from service at your former company, you should apply for unemployment benefits. If you wait too long, you may make yourself ineligible because you didn't apply soon enough. Even if you are under the impression that your severance will count as wages, and that you will therefore not be able to collect unemployment until after you have received all your severance pay, you should file right away. The state will then note that your claim has been made within the required time period, and you will not risk missing the deadline that your state mandates. It is also imperative that you are completely honest in the information you provide on the forms that you file. Anything less could jeopardize your eligibility.

Here's the bottom line: there are three keys regarding unemployment. Number one, the benefits are an insurance program. Your employer paid into the insurance program and you should not feel guilty whatsoever about collecting benefits. Number two, your pension, if it comes from the same company that issued your layoff, could cancel your unemployment benefit - so be careful as you make a decision about when to begin your pension. Number three, you need to file with the appropriate state unemployment agency right away, as soon as you have been laid off, so as not to miss a critical deadline.

Chapter 3

What Do I Do about Health Insurance?

The cost of health insurance is far and away the most often cited reason for people deciding not to retire early, electing to delay retirement to age 65. Many clients I've worked with over the years have been ready to retire at age 62 or 63 and have had sufficient savings to retire at that age or, in some cases, even earlier. Then they realize that if they retire early, they will have to bear the brunt of health insurance costs and pay for their health insurance. That changes the timetable. Let's walk through how and why.

Unquestionably, one of the biggest obstacles to retiring

before age 65 is finding affordable health insurance. At age 65, you are eligible to receive Medicare, so it is bridging the gap up until age 65 that is most challenging, especially if you are unexpectedly forced to retire. It takes a considerable amount of effort, and can be extremely expensive, to purchase health insurance.

Most workers will not receive any retiree health insurance from their former employer. In fact, only 28 percent of large companies with 200 or more workers offer any kind of health insurance in retirement. That statistic is from 2010; the percentage is most likely even smaller today. Even among companies that do provide retiree health benefits, they are able to increase your out-of-pocket costs – and frequently do – or even revoke your benefits. So even if you anticipate receiving health insurance from your former company in retirement, it may not be guaranteed. You need to proceed very carefully.

There are now a number of options available for you to consider.

The most recent option to be introduced is under the Affordable Care Act (ACA), often referred to as ObamaCare, which includes an early retiree reinsurance program. Under the program, states and companies offer early retirement coverage and get reimbursement from the federal government. The average cost for a retiree under age 65 for that program is $633.00 per month; but the company is going to subsidize that and ask for a reimbursement. Here's what you need to know: if you receive an early retirement offer, or you're forced to retire early, you should anticipate about $600.00 to $700.00 per month, per person, for full health insurance through the age of 65.

Another option is going on what is known as COBRA. COBRA coverage means that you actually stay on your employer's health insurance, but you pay your entire premium for that coverage. Let's say you're offered early retirement at age 63-and-a-half. You can elect to go on COBRA for as long as 18 months, which in this scenario would cover you all the way until age 65. If you haven't quite reached age 63-and-a-half and you are forced to retire, you could go on COBRA for as long as you need to before you are able to find other health insurance coverage.

There is another option if you have a spouse that is

working and health insurance is available through your spouse's employer. Upon being laid off and facing the abrupt end of your health insurance coverage, you could immediately apply to be added to that health insurance plan with your spouse. You do not need to wait for an open enrollment period – typically in the fall or spring - at your spouse's employer. Even if it is the middle of the year, you can apply for coverage under your spouse's health insurance, and you would be added, because being laid off is considered to be a "triggering event" which allows such changes outside of open enrollment periods.

Pretend for a moment that I have been laid off, there is no health insurance available to me, I do not have a spouse's plan to join, and COBRA is completely unaffordable for me. Through the Affordable Care Act, if I meet certain income thresholds, I may be eligible to receive tax credits that could cover up to 100 percent of the premium.

Under ACA, if your income is less than $46,000.00 per year for an individual, for example, you could qualify for a tax credit that may end up covering almost all of your health insurance coverage. To find out, either go on the federal www.healthcare.gov website or your state's website, which may be a different site. (Connecticut's website is www.accesshealthct.com; Massachusetts' website is www.mahealthconnector.org)

At the website, enter the information that is requested and the site will provide you with a quote for the cost of coverage, based on your income. One of the determining factors, therefore, will be your estimate of your retirement income. If you are going to pull money out of an IRA or a 401(k), that will be added to your income. If you are going to collect Social Security early, that will also be added to your income. So, the quote you receive will be based on the data you input.

The Affordable Care Act has changed the landscape. Health insurance is much more readily available now, where previously you had to go out and find your own insurance. Before ACA, there could be pre-existing conditions that would eliminate you from being able to get health insurance. That is no longer true with ACA.

For a person facing sudden retirement, or who is

considering retiring early before age 65, the cost of health insurance remains a significant issue. It is probably going to cost you some extra money - most likely until when you are age 65 and you can go on Medicare. The key to keeping that cost down is keeping your income sufficiently low for those first few years. Fortunately, there are ways to do that. There are annuity strategies, for example, where you can receive money every month, but it is not considered to be taxable income and therefore is not added to your income level. If you are able to determine strategies that would allow you to qualify for some of the ACA subsidies, then it may be possible for you to be insured without the costs being as financially painful.

The moral of this section of the story is that if you are considering retirement, whether by choice or because you were laid off, this should be part of a comprehensive retirement review that you undertake with a qualified, certified financial planner - where you can look at all of the issues discussed in this book, and make an informed decision about whether you can afford not to work or whether you have to go back to work, and what to do about your health insurance.

Chapter 4

When Should I Take Social Security?

Here is the age-old question: "When should I begin taking my Social Security?" As most of you know, Social Security is a federal program that is funded through payroll taxes, and it is available when you turn age 62. If you qualify for Social Security payments, you can begin taking Social Security – receiving a monthly benefit check - as early as age 62.

Retirement age is a somewhat different question, and one that you may be less familiar with. In terms of retirement age, for purposes of Social Security, if you were born between 1943 and 1954, the retirement age is 66. If you were born after 1960, it's age 67. Most of the clients that we work with were born between 1943 and 1960, so the "normal retirement age," in accordance with

Social Security Administration guidelines, is between age 66 and 67.

What does "normal retirement age" mean? That is the age when you qualify for what is considered to be your full social security benefit. Here's how the process works: If you take Social Security at age 62, which is legally permissible, there would to be a reduction in your social security benefit of approximately 25 percent. So, for example, if my benefit would have been $2,000.00 a month at my full retirement age and I opt to take begin taking Social Security at age 62, instead of receiving $2,000.00 a month, I will receive $1,500.00 per month - reflecting the 25 percent reduction. Again, keep in mind that full retirement age is 67 if you were born after 1960, and 66 if you were born between 1943 and 1954. (For those born between 1954 and 1959, the normal retirement age is between 66 and 67.)

The main point here is not to focus on precisely what the reduction would be, but the more important concept that *the earlier you take Social Security, the smaller your monthly checks will be.*

Joel M. Johnson

The equation works both ways – the longer you delay beginning Social Security after your normal retirement age, the larger your monthly checks will be. You can delay taking Social Security until age 70. If you are able to delay taking Social Security until age 70, you will receive a much larger benefit than you would have received if you began at your full retirement age.

Here's another way to view the impact of your choice on when to begin taking Social Security: if you retire at age 62 and take Social Security, you might get only half as much as you would if you waited until age 70. That is a concept worth repeating, and underscores how the decision you make on when to begin taking Social Security can have a dramatic impact on the amount of the check you'll receive every month. It comes down to this: *the longer I wait, the larger my monthly checks.*

FULL RETIREMENT AND AGE 62 BENEFIT BY YEAR OF BIRTH[3]

Year of Birth[1]	Full (normal) Retirement Age	Months between age 62 and full retirement age[2]	A $1000 retirement benefit would be reduced to	The retirement benefit is reduced by[4]	A $500 spouses's benefit would be reduced to	The spouses's benefit is reduced by[3]
1937 or earlier	65	36	$800	20.00%	$375	25.00%
1938	65 and 2 months	38	$791	20.83%	$370	25.83%
1939	65 and 4 months	40	$783	21.67%	$366	26.67%
1940	65 and 6 months	42	$775	22.50%	$362	27.50%
1941	65 and 8 months	44	$766	23.33%	$358	28.33%
1942	65 and 10 months	46	$758	24.17%	$354	29.17%
1943-1954	66	48	$750	25.00%	$350	30.00%
1955	66 and 2 months	50	$741	25.83%	$345	30.83%
1956	66 and 4 months	52	$733	26.67%	$341	31.67%
1957	66 and 6 months	54	$725	27.50%	$337	32.50%
1958	66 and 8 months	56	$716	28.33%	$333	33.33%
1959	66 and 10 months	58	$708	29.17%	$329	34.17%
1960 and later	67	60	$700	30.00%	$325	35.00%

Take a look at the accompanying chart that shows your full retirement age and the reduction for taking Social Security at age 62. It is easy to use. Just find your year of birth along the left side and then look at what the impact would be if you decide to take Social Security at age 62. For instance, if I was born in 1957, the chart indicates that my "normal retirement age" would be at age 66-and-six-months. A $1,000.00 retirement benefit if I retire at age 66-and-six-months would be substantially reduced if I take it beginning at age 62 – I would receive $725.00 a month.

That illustrates why it is very important to make your decision regarding when to begin taking Social Security within the context of a full retirement income plan. When developed by an expert, a retirement income plan will answer critical questions that should be considered, such as "what are your other retirement sources?" and "can I afford to delay taking Social Security until I would receive a larger benefit?"

There is one more important factor to consider: just because your monthly check is larger does not necessarily mean that you are going to get more money. That's because you don't know how long you are going to live.

Let's walk through that, briefly. If I take Social Security at age 62 and I die at age 70, I'm going to get much more money, in total, out of the system in those eight years (between age 62 and 70) than I would if I had opted to wait until I was 66 to begin taking Social Security. If I wait until I'm 66, my monthly check will be larger, but I would have given up four years of monthly checks between age 62 and 66, so my cumulative total by age 70 will be less. Thus, the longer you wait, the larger your monthly checks - but that doesn't mean you're going to receive more money in Social Security benefit payments.

Ultimately, whether you are going to get more money out of the system is dependent upon how long you are going to live. That can be estimated by considering family history, life history, and life expectancy - how long your parents or siblings lived (or their current age), and whether there are health issues that may be a factor.

There are also a number of other strategies that may be available to you. One possibility is that you could trigger a benefit under a spousal provision within the Social Security system. For instance, if my wife and I are both age 66, I could in effect draw some benefits from her benefits. In this approach, she could take her full benefit, and I would take half of her benefit, for example, thereby allowing my Social Security benefit to continue to accrue until I am age 70, when I would trigger my benefits. Another aspect to understand is whether survivor benefits for one of you is considerably higher than for the other. That should be factored into your decision.

Overall, be aware that if you take Social Security before your full retirement age, you may lock yourself out of some other potentially beneficial options, especially if you're married.

There is an additional option that you should be aware of - the provision of a widow or widower's benefit. If you were married to someone for ten years and they passed away, you could trigger a Social Security benefit when you are 60 years old. Obviously, not everyone is eligible for this, but for those who are, it is an option to consider. If you were married for ten years and divorced, you may be able to collect under your ex-spouse's benefit. You would not receive benefits at age 60, as would a widow or widower, but you could collect at age 62.

So, when should you take Social Security? There is no one-size-fits-all answer. That's why having a comprehensive Social Security analysis developed by an expert, such as a Certified Financial Planner, is in your best interest. As has been highlighted in this chapter:

- When you begin taking Social Security can have substantial financial consequences, and there are a range of influences, such as normal retirement age and other retirement income resources, that come into play.
- There are "tricks of the trade" options that can help you to maximize your Social Security benefit.

- There needs to be an educated "best guess" on your life expectancy.

The last time I checked, there were more than 500 different combinations and different ways to take Social Security. Before determining a course of action, you should have your specific situation carefully analyzed so that you can make the best Social Security decision for you.

Chapter 5

When Should I Take My Pension?

As with Social Security, the decision you make as to when you will take your pension – as well as your decision regarding survivor benefits - is very important, and no two situations are alike. Most pensions have many options and combinations that typically cannot be changed once chosen. There is one noteworthy difference from Social Security - not all pensions increase if you delay taking your benefit.

In this chapter, the focus will be on various types of pensions and the choices you will have at retirement. Among the critical questions: "Should I take monthly payments for life or should I take a lump sum and roll it over into a IRA?" To illustrate the possibilities, I will share a real-life example of a choice that a client had to make, and how we were able to assist the decision-making process based on his, and his wife's, specific situation.

Let's begin with the idea behind, and the benefits of, a pension. Back when my grandfather and my father were working, pensions were extremely popular, and almost every company offered a pension plan to its employees. The fundamental idea was to reward workers for staying with the company for a very long time. The approach was generally described in this way: "If you work for us for the next 20 to 30 years and you retire at age 65, we promise that you will get a monthly check that is guaranteed to continue for as long as you live. And if you are willing to reduce your monthly check just slightly, we'll even guarantee that that check comes into your home for as long as you or your wife lives."

That approach sounds somewhat like Social Security, in that you work for a certain amount of time and you receive a check that arrives every month. The fundamental difference between Social Security and a pension, of course, is that pensions are basically guaranteed by a company, where Social Security comes directly from the United States government. (There is a limited federal insurance guaranteeing the pension.) Thus, while not at the level of certainty of Social Security, there is a substantial financial security with a pension.

Most pensions start at age 65, or they're designed to start at age 65. Here is an example: I can retire at age 65 and receive a check for $3,000.00 a month that is guaranteed for as long as I live. Or, I can take a check for somewhat less, $2,700.00 a month, but if I die before my wife, then she would receive approximately half of my benefits for the remainder of her life. There is, in effect, some longevity insurance that I purchase by giving up part of my pension. I receive less each month, but if I die before my spouse, she would continue to receive a monthly benefit.

A few years back, there was a very popular option where an individual would take the differential - in that example, $300.00 per month - and consider how much life insurance could be purchased for $300.00 Then, instead of taking $2,700.00 a month and assuring that their spouse would continue to receive payments after their death from the pension, they would take the full amount of that differential, $300.00 a month, and purchase a life insurance policy on their spouse. Upon the pension recipient's death, that life insurance policy would produce income for the surviving spouse.

That scenario is known as "pension max" in the life insurance business, and serves to maximize the pension. The benefit of buying the insurance policy is that if the spouse of the pension recipient dies first, the insurance policy can be dropped or cashed in, and the pension recipient would receive $3,000.00 a month for their rest of their life instead of $2,700.00. Since most people cannot accurately predict which spouse will die first, the "pension max" approach presents a sound alternative as you begin retirement.

The other option that is often offered through pension plans today is the option to roll over a lump sum instead of taking a monthly benefit. Using the previous example of $3,000.00 a month, a pension plan administrator may say, "We're going to pay you $3,000.00 a month for the rest of your life beginning at age 65, or you can have a $600,000.00 lump sum benefit, and we won't pay you anything every month. We just give you the lump sum and you're on your own to invest it."

In our financial services practice, we frequently discuss the importance of flexibility and control. If you elect to take that lump sum, it gives you the ability, as a retiree, to control the way the money is invested. You give up the monthly guarantee that's offered to you by the company. But instead of a $3,000.00 a month guarantee, you now have $600,000.00 that you can invest on my own, as you choose to invest it.

If you do some basic math, you'll figure out that $600,000.00 at six percent equals $3,000.00 a month. Here's what that means. If you can earn six percent on that money, you can create your own $3,000.00 a month - and have control over the principal. You would be taking some risk, by removing the guarantee from the company. But instead, you would have control over the principal.

Think for a moment about what that control can offer. For example, what if you do not need the full $3,000.00 a month. You can take slightly less and let the remaining lump sum grow - again, assuming that you are earning six percent. What if from time-to-time you want extra money out of the lump sum, maybe to purchase a car or to take the kids and grandkids on a vacation. Let's say you want an extra $25,000.00 one year to splurge on a vacation for the kids and grandkids. If you have the control and flexibility, you are able to remove that from the lump sum as you wish.

Keep in mind that you would need to roll over the lump sum into an IRA, otherwise, as we have discussed, it would be taxable all at once. But once the lump sum pension at retirement has been rolled over into an IRA, you would then have control over the entire lump sum, how it is invested, and when and how you take your money out.

Here is another scenario to think about. What if my wife and I die five years after I've retired? If I had opted to take the pension, regardless of the option selected, the income would stop and the kids and grandkids would inherit nothing, zero. My church or synagogue would get nothing, the organizations that I care about from a charitable perspective would get nothing. In effect, I would have left a substantial amount of money – money that could have benefitted family or charitable organizations - in the company, because I only received five years worth of $3,000.00 a month payments.

In the alternative, if I elected to take the lump sum and my wife and I pass away after five years, whatever remains in the IRA can go to my kids, my grandkids, and my charity. I can direct that it be split it up any number of different ways. As this example demonstrates, control is significant factor from the standpoint of having the ability, at some future date, to pass forward your remaining money, in accordance with your wishes.

Most clients, when faced with this choice and for the reasons cited, elect to take the lump sum. A smaller percentage of clients take the monthly option. Those that take the monthly payments tend to do so for one of two main reasons:

- At times, the monthly option offers a very high rate of return compared to the lump sum and or is simply an approach they are more comfortable with. We don't see that as often, but it does occur from time-to-time.

- The other reason is that they are apprehensive about their own ability to control spending, or they are concerned that when they pass away their spouse will not be able to handle such a large amount of money properly (and they have not set up a trust or estate planning to have that money managed properly). In these circumstances, they may prefer to have the peace of mind of knowing that that $3,000.00 a month is going to come in for the rest of their lives.

Considering A Real-Life Example

Let's examine a real-life scenario from our financial planning practice a few years ago. We will refer to this hypothetical couple – based on real circumstances – as Bob and Betty.

(turn to the next page for the chart & example)

I have included a chart that highlights Bob and Betty's options – choices that Bob was faced with when he retired from an engineering firm where he had worked for 30 years. As you see on the chart entitled "Pension Estimates," one option that he had was to take a lump sum at age 62 of $484,276.80. You can see that because the voluntary lump sum option on the chart is bolded.

Slightly farther down are the different options he could take as a pension. You can see that he could take a life annuity of $3,104.00 per month. If you look just over to the right of that, you will notice that his surviving beneficiary, Betty, would get zero if he died first.

If you look further down that column, where you can see his pension choices, you will notice that he could also take what is described as 67 percent joint and survivor with an increase, which means that he could start out receiving $2,678.67 a month; and if he died, his wife would receive $1,785.87 per month for the rest of her life. He was leaning towards this option until we examined what could be done if he took the lump sum of $484,276.80 and rolled it over into an IRA.

Pension Estimates		
Stop Working	62 yrs 0 mos	06/30/2012
Benefit Commencement	62 yrs 0 mos	07/01/2012
Beneficiary	Spouse	
Beneficiary Date of Birth	07/25/1952	
Salary Increase per year	0.0%	
Bonus Amount Paid per year	$15,000.00	
Available Options	Scenario 1	
	You	**Spouse**
Cash Balance Plan		
Voluntary Lump Sum	$484,276.80 Lump Sum	N/A
Life Annuity	$3,104.56 Monthly	N/A
100% Joint and Survivor Annuity with Increase	$2,526.93 Monthly	$2,526.93 Monthly
50% Joint and Survivor Annuity with Increase	$2,761.59 Monthly	$1,380.80 Monthly
67% Joint & Survivor with Increase	**$2,678.67 Monthly**	**$1,785.87 Monthly**
75% Joint and Survivor Annuity with Increase	$2,639.05 Monthly	$1,979.29 Monthly
5 Year Certain and Continuous	$3,044.30 Monthly	$3,044.30 Monthly
10 Year Certain and Continuous	$2,898.44 Monthly	$2,898.44 Monthly
15 Year Certain and Continuous	$2,722.84 Monthly	$2,722.84 Monthly
20 Year Certain and Continuous	$2,553.85 Monthly	$2,553.85 Monthly

Forced to Retire

Before we move ahead to the final decision there, let's look at his Social Security option.

Betty was a school teacher, and in the state of Connecticut, school teachers do not get their full Social Security benefit. That is because their paycheck, as teachers, is not reduced to have money paid into Social Security. But in a sense, it can be considered a penalty (referred to as the "Windfall Provision") because even if Betty worked outside the school system, she still does not get her full Social Security credits.

Social Security	At 62	At 66	At 70
Male	$1,814	$2,450	$3,261
Female	$293	$389	$514

You will see in the chart that Bob, at age 62, could get $1,814.00 a month, and Betty, at age 62, could get $293.00 a month. Then you will notice precisely what we highlighted in the previous chapter about Social Security. If Bob waits until age 66, he would receive a higher benefit; and if he waits until age 70, he would receive a substantially higher benefit, and Betty's benefit increases as well.

It is important to remember that usually if the husband in such a scenario waits and takes his benefit at age 70, his wife, upon the death of her husband, can step right into

that survivor's benefit. But because Betty was a school teacher in Connecticut, that benefit is not available. So what we elected to do, in consultation with our client, was quite interesting, and underscores that everyone's circumstance is different.

First of all, Bob elected to take Social Security immediately, at age 62. Betty is getting her teacher's pension. What that does is it makes sure that if Bob should die early, they will not have left money in the system, because Betty is not able to assume his social security benefit.

We also conducted an analysis of Bob's assets outside the pension, and learned that he had a substantial 401(k) with approximately $1 million in it. So we decided with him that he would take the voluntary lump sum, roll it into an IRA, and together with his 401(k) it created a balance of about $1.5 million. From that $1.5 million, Bob receives $3,000.00 a month, from his combined 401(k) and pension lump sum, now in an IRA.

He is getting his Social Security, Betty is getting a small Social Security check plus a teacher's pension, and they determined that would be enough for them to not only get by, but afford to do some things they hope to do. Bob also has various mutual funds outside of what is shown here, and he triggered some income from those mutual funds. That income was not from his IRA, and some was tax-free.

What we were able to do with Bob and Betty, first and foremost, is take control, as we have discussed, by his electing to receive the lump sum instead of taking the payout. Even though the payout number is somewhat attractive, approximately seven percent, he did not really need all the income on a monthly basis that they were offering from the pension; and he preferred to have control over the lump sum.

Secondly, he now has all the flexibility. He has his 401(k) and the pension plan; it has all been rolled over into one pot. It has been allocated under a wonderful investment program, in which he has a portion of the money in safe indexed annuities that have guaranteed income in the future, and he's taking some income from that.

Additionally, he has a portion of the money in what we call "steady income tools," such as Real Estate Trusts and Private Equity Loan Programs, and he has some money exposed in the traditional stock and bond, mutual fund, and exchange-traded fund portfolios that we typically build for clients.

With that blend, we are expecting (of course, there is no guarantee of future results) a rate of return on that retirement money of six to seven percent net of all expenses which is more than enough to generate what would have been the pension income, and now he has control over the entire lump sum.

As this chapter's discussion - and this scenario – indicates, the pension decision is very, very important. It is perhaps even more crucial than the Social Security decision. The critical aspect to remember is that everybody's situation is unique.

As someone who is either facing a retirement decision or has already faced a retirement decision but hasn't yet made a choice regarding their pension, it is imperative to sit down with an individual who is very knowledgeable and qualified, such as a certified financial planner.

This individual should also act as a fiduciary, which means they are required to act in your best interest to make the right pension decision in conjunction with Social Security and other assets to build the retirement program that's appropriate for you.

Chapter 6

401(k): Leave It or Roll It Over to an IRA?

This may be a relatively basic decision and an area that you are largely aware of, but it is worth walking through just to be sure – and there may be some nuances you are not familiar with. When it comes to the question of what to do with the 401(k) at the company that you are leaving, the theme of flexibility and control, once again, is key.

A 401(k) is a retirement savings plan, sponsored by an employer, which provides employees with an opportunity to save and invest a portion of their paycheck before taxes are taken out. Generally, taxes aren't paid until the money is withdrawn from the account.

The regulations pertaining to 401(k) accounts allow you to roll money over - move the funds - when there is what is referred to as a "triggering event." That can be a separation from service from your company, or you reach age 59-and-a-half, or it could be disability or death. Let's just focus on two of those triggering events - separation from service from your company or reaching a certain age.

If you leave a company, the federal government requires that the company allow you to roll over your 401(k) to another financial vehicle, anywhere you'd like. You are also permitted to cash it in. The problem with cashing it in, however, is you would owe taxes on all the money immediately, so that is not an attractive option. You could, however, roll the money over to an Individual Retirement Account (IRA).

Age can also be a triggering event. At some major employers, you are able to roll over the 401(k) to an IRA at anytime, even while you are still working for the company, once you reach a certain age. That age may be 50, or 55, or 59½, and varies from company to company. Virtually every large employer - companies such as United Technologies, the Hartford, AT&T, Boeing, General Motors – permit you, once you reach age 59½, to roll over your 401(k) to an IRA, even if you are still working for the company.

The advantage of this is flexibility and control. Here's why. If you roll your 401(k) over to an IRA, you are now able to invest it in any way that you choose; you are not limited to selecting from the investment menu of the 401(k) provider. This would allow you, for example, to buy annuities which would guarantee your principal. You could move your funds to an indexed annuity where when the market goes up, you would benefit, but when the market goes down, you would not lose money. Any gains - if you have gains in any given year - can be locked in.

That's a pretty neat account, and one that I own – in fact, I actually own two index annuities. I can buy real estate trusts or private equity funds that I can't get inside the 401(k) because of the structure of those investments. And typically, I can continue to buy all the same mutual funds that I can buy inside the 401(k).

Let me add a couple of notes about buying mutual funds outside the 401(k) versus inside. Sometimes the fees are lower on the funds I can buy outside the 401(k) than those that are offered inside the 401(k), and sometimes the 401(k) has very inexpensive mutual funds that I can buy where it's actually a better deal than buying the funds outside the 401(k). So it is important to consult with an expert when it comes to funds that are inside, versus outside, of the 401(k).

The point in all of this is to achieve flexibility and control. That is why most of our clients, as soon as they can, roll over at least a portion - if not all - of their 401(k) to an IRA. That allows us to structure a better investment program for them.

There is one circumstance where you would not want to roll your 401(k) over to an IRA – that would be if you retire before age 59½. The IRS actually says that it is permissible to pull money out of a 401(k) at 55 and not be subject to the ten percent extra IRS penalty. However, as soon as that money moves to an IRA, if you have not reached age 59½, those funds would instantly be subject to the age 59½ rule – and you could not withdraw money without it being subject to the IRS penalty.

Let's say I am 56-years-old when I retire from a large company, and I know that I will need some income before I turn 59½. My financial situation is such that I cannot wait for age 59½. In this situation, I might choose to leave some of my 401(k) funds behind in the 401(k) from the company from which I am retiring, because it will enable me to create an income stream which will fill the gap in my finances until age 59½. At that time, I can tap into my IRA without the extra penalty from the IRS. That is basically the only circumstance in which it would make sense to leave money behind in a 401(k).

In the old days – when I say the old days, I mean five or six years ago – there were some attractive guaranteed accounts that you could consider for your 401(k) that would pay six, seven, even eight percent interest. They were called "stable value accounts." Unfortunately, those just don't exist anymore. The best stable value account I know of, as of the writing of this book, pays 3½ percent – which makes it much less attractive to leave money behind in a 401(k).

This brief discussion of 401(k)'s, and whether to roll the money over or leave it in an IRA, has hopefully helped to clarify your choices. Most of all, I hope you recognize that under current rules that provide the protection of an IRA, it makes a lot of sense to roll money out of the 401(k) as soon as possible into an IRA. You may also want to consider consolidating several 401(k)'s into one, as part of developing a sound and simple investment strategy that will benefit you and your family.

Chapter 7

How Do I Invest My Retirement Nest Egg?

We have walked through all of the critical decisions that must be made when you learn that you're being forced to retire, or are offered a retirement package. They all lead to another equally significant question that must be answered: "can I actually afford to retire?" That is especially pivotal if you are considering doing something else when you leave the company, or if you are thinking about completely retiring.

Let's say that after making all the decisions outlined in the previous chapters, you arrive at a point where you say, "Okay, I can retire." The follow-up questions are: "How do I invest that retirement nest egg? How do I make sure that my needs are met?"

There are two major aspects that will allow you to arrive at an answer:

- Creating what is called a "Retirement Income Plan" or a "Retirement Income Analysis." This was briefly described in a previous chapter, and is something we develop for almost all of our clients.

- Determining the proper use of various investment tools to create the rate of return that you want (and need).

Let's discuss each of them.

Retirement Income Plan

I earnestly believe that every person facing retirement should have a retirement income plan - and almost everybody is facing retirement, sooner or later. A retirement income plan includes the income that you want coming into your house every month throughout your retirement, and then it lines up the guaranteed sources of income that you anticipate you will have – such as Social Security and pensions.

If there is a shortfall between the income you want and

the guaranteed sources of income you anticipate, we then look at those investments to determine how can we create an investment program to fill the gap to make up for the retirement income shortfall.

Let's look at the chart below that illustrates how this would work. Suppose we have determined that you would need $10,000.00 a month, but between you and your spouse your household will receive $4,500.00 a month, including Social Security and pensions. That leaves you with a $5,500.00 a month shortfall. Next, we would look at your investable assets to determine how we can produce that additional $5,500.00 a month. The analysis will indicate whether you have sufficient savings to last for the rest of your life or if you are likely to fall short.

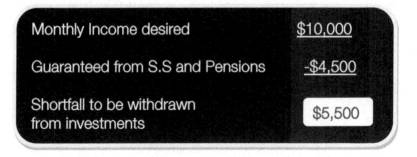

Monthly Income desired	$10,000
Guaranteed from S.S and Pensions	-$4,500
Shortfall to be withdrawn from investments	$5,500

There will be some people who have enough money

invested to last not only for the rest of their life, but also enables them to leave something behind for someone they love. Most people, however, will fall short. That leads to a discussion evaluating how to increase the rate of return on the investment portfolio, or, in the alternative, the possibility of dialing back slightly on the $10,000.00 a month objective. The retirement income plan is going to provide us with a roadmap for decision-making.

In developing your plan, it is also important to remember to include raises each year to keep up with inflation. This is something we include when building a retirement plan for our clients. We build in a 3% increase every year to keep up with the cost of living.

One of the most valuable aspects of the retirement income plan is that it tells us the rate of return that will be required to get your investment nest egg to produce the results that you want for the rest of your life. Some people need to get a six, seven, or eight percent rate of return. Other people only need a four or five percent rate of return.

If you are among those who require a four or five percent

rate of return, you can achieve that with very, very low risk. Yet, if you start talking about your portfolio with a stock broker or someone from one of the big brokerage firms - who generally have a bias toward putting a lot of your money in the stock market - you might end up taking on more risk than you'd prefer. Not good, and not necessary.

Don't let anybody talk you into taking more risk than you're comfortable with. You should be the driver of your investment philosophy. You should be dealing with a professional that you are comfortable with. And you should be working with someone who understands that preservation of principle is usually the most important priority driving investment decisions in retirement.

Let's say we did a retirement income plan for you and determined that you need a five percent rate of return. Our focus then turns to exploring which financial vehicles could provide that five percent rate of return. We might, for example, examine annuities which offer a guaranteed income stream for as long as you live. It doesn't even matter what the underlying account earns. The key is the guaranteed income for as long as you live – it is almost like going out and buying your own pension.

In the alternative, if your preference is to stay away from annuities because of the time commitment they require, we might move toward developing an investment portfolio. Basically, it comes down to a choice between guaranteed sources of income or taking some risk for a potentially higher rate of return and additional flexibility. Either way, whatever you decide is right for you should be the direction that your financial advisor travels.

Investment   *Tools*

To begin our discussion of the use of various investment tools, I direct your attention to the accompanying chart. The chart is in a circle, split three ways.

1) The category on the upper-right is the "*market*," which represents anything that we can buy that trades in the market. That would include a stock, a bond, a stock fund or bond fund, an exchange-traded fund, a closed-end mutual fund – anything that can be traded everyday. The advantage of that sector is that even with a diversified portfolio, we could make up to 40 percent or more in a given year. The disadvantage, of course, is that we could lose up to 40 percent or more in a given year.

   Another advantage of the market portfolio is that it is very flexible; it is totally liquid. I can pull money out at any time, add money, or make adjustments as needs arise. There are clear advantages and disadvantages of the market portfolio, but many people are less comfortable with the market portfolio when they have retired because they don't believe there would be sufficient time for their portfolio to make up for a market downturn.

2) On the upper left is the "*steady income*" category. These are investment programs and strategies where financial advisors invest your money with the goal of generating approximately a six to eight percent steady return - hence the name "steady income." These investments are illiquid. When we go into these investments, one of the catches is that we have to leave money there for three to five years; some of them even longer than that.

The tradeoff for that illiquidity is an investment program that's designed to provide a return of six to eight percent, plus all your principal, at the end of that three to five-year period. It doesn't go up-and-down with the stock market, and most of these investments - such as real estate or private equity funds - are not subject to the fluxuations of the market for their rate of return. If you own a portfolio of real estate and the tenants are companies like Wal-Mart and Home Depot, for example, you can be quite certain that they are going to pay their rent. (If they are unable to, the economy has much bigger problems.) As rents continue to come in with predictability and reliability, you benefit from that, and it is the basis for the six-seven percent cash flow. But again, it is illiquid and there is no guarantee of principal or return of your money.

However, what if you blended the "steady income" category with the "market" category in order to smooth out rates of return? The result may be a very attractive rate of return, without taking on all the risk of the stock market. This strategy isn't right for everybody, but it does provide a glimpse of the various options that are available – something that many brokers won't even talk about. In fact, there are some very famous brokers that publish material advising people never to invest in these areas. The reason, quite simply, is because of their own limitations - they only operate in "the market."

3)   At the bottom is the category called "*safe*," which means we cannot lose principal – there is some type of a guarantee. This was mentioned earlier in the book when "annuities" were referenced. What is confusing about annuities is that there are actually four different types. Certain types of annuities offer protection of principal, no

matter what. In that type, even if the insurance company fails there is a "state guarantee fund" that guarantees your principal. It is not FDIC insurance, it is your state that stands behind that guarantee fund. There is also a protection of principal with U.S. government bonds because they are guaranteed by the federal government.

Of course, we can also put money in bank deposits because they have FDIC protection.

The three categories of investment tools to be considered are *market*, *steady income* and *safe*. If we have determined in doing a retirement income analysis that you need a five or six percent rate of return, we can blend those three categories together and provide you with what we expect will be a very nice income stream, very low risk (much lower than by trying to achieve that return solely with mutual funds or stocks and bonds) and the flexibility that you need to take extra money out from time-to-time.

What is also particularly valuable about this approach is that it provides an ability to leave the *market* piece alone when the market goes down, giving it time to recover, because we can take our income from the other two pieces of the portfolio, *steady income* and *safe.*

Another important aspect to understand as you look at this chart is that it is not intended to convey that we recommend you do one-third, one-third, one-third split – that is not true at all, it is merely how the chart appears. It is the proper blending of these three categories in the proper percentages - unique to you and your family - that spell success in this particular strategy. The blending is the key.

You should also keep in mind – as we do – that all of these pieces are not necessarily right for everybody. The *steady income* piece may not be right for you. The *market* piece may not be right because you may not want any exposure to the stock market. Or the *safe* piece may not be right for you because of the strings attached - most insurance companies require some type of a time commitment. (Right now, insurance companies offer the most attractive returns in that safe category.)

You have to be completely comfortable with the strings attached before you proceed into that particular investment category.

Let me share some personal examples. As of the writing of this book, I have money in all of these categories. My father only has money in *market* and *safe* because he is somewhat apprehensive about real estate; he just always has been. My mother-in-law has money in *safe* and in *steady income*, but very little in the *market*. All of which illustrates three unique situations within one family – me, my dad, and my mother-in-law.

In those situations, we have unique individuals with different needs and different levels of comfort with various investments. As you consider how best to invest your retirement nest egg, hopefully this chapter has helped to open your eyes to the range of possibilities.

Forced to Retire

Note from the Author

I appreciate your having this book in hand and taking the time to read about some of the ways we have helped clients at Johnson Brunetti respond to an imminent – and often unanticipated – retirement.

For many people, especially in recent times, retirement has come as a bolt from the blue, unexpected and uninvited. For others, it is not a shock. It is a consideration that has been in the back of your mind for a while, but uncertainty about whether you are financially able to retire has prevented you from moving forward. Even under the best of circumstances, the financial decisions surrounding retirement can be confusing and perplexing.

We have extensive experience working with retirees in a wide range of circumstances, and much of the wisdom that we offer comes from understanding what other retirees have gone through as they enter their retirement life. Knowing the critical questions that need to be answered and decisions that need to be made, having the expertise to guide prospective or sudden

retirees through their options, and recognizing the importance of treating each individuals' situation as unique, all combine to provide us with the background and perspective that can be most helpful at what is often a trying time.

Certainly, there are many other financial advisors that work with retirees; I would encourage you to find a professional that you are comfortable with, and that specializes in precisely where you are at this particular stage of your life.

Once again, I want to thank you for picking up this book, and taking a look. Please keep the seven questions that we have discussed in mind as you respond to the challenges ahead. Hopefully this has been very helpful for you, and the material has been presented in a way that is both easy to understand and offers useful insight.

We appreciate you and the trust you've placed in our Firm.

Forced to Retire

Bonus

How to Find the Right Financial Advisor

Here are nine important points you should keep in mind when you try to find the correct financial advisor. It is important that there is "chemistry" between you, that there is a good fit and a sharing of values. There also should be a feeling that the person understands you.

1. Independent

It is very important that the financial advisor you choose be independent, someone who is not an employee of a large firm. There are many firms at which brokers and advisors can work. I started in the business 26 years ago as an employee of a big brokerage firm, and we employees were told what products and funds to recommend. We were told that what we had to sell was perfect for everyone. When our sales manager had certain stocks that he would decide we should push in a certain month, guess what? Those stocks were what most people ended up owning.

I soon came to realize that this was the wrong approach, but unfortunately it still goes on today. Let's take, for example, a very large Wall Street brokerage firm. First of all, if you work for such a firm, the people you work with are employees of that firm, so their primary responsibility is to that firm, not to you. Their job is to increase shareholder value for that particular firm. You're just a customer.

However, if you work with an independent financial advisor, then you are the only person to whom that advisor answers. An ethical independent financial advisor does not have an agenda or a list of stocks to push. It is very important that you find an independent financial advisor.

2. Chemistry

The second important consideration is "chemistry." It's very important that you feel the person you're talking to understands you. If you are a husband and wife, make sure the person talks to both of you and also listens to both of you. If for one moment you feel that a broker is dismissing you or your feelings or is insulting or is coming across as arrogant, this is the wrong person to work with. You need to choose an advisor who understands you, who listens to you, and who will put together a financial plan that fits your needs and goals.

3. Empathy

Does the advisor understand you and feel like you do when it comes to your important issues? You may have a special-needs child who requires special planning. You may come from a very poor family, one that lived through the depression, and you're worried about running out of money. Can that advisor relate? It's critical that the advisor listen and feel empathy for your particular fears. Another clue that you're working with the wrong advisor is he or she does not understand or does not listen.

4. Adequate Staffing

Staffing is a critical issue: it's where the rubber meets the road in today's financial world. Make sure the advisor you work with has plenty of service staff, and do so by simply asking. I know some firms where a broker handles hundreds of accounts without a full-time assistant or maybe sharing one with another broker. This isn't going to work very well. Two things can happen.

Number one, the service level drops; number two, the broker or advisor has to constantly answer every phone call, every service inquiry. If I am talking to my advisor, I want one who is thinking about my investments, one who deals one-on-one with clients, not one bogged down by service inquiries and other issues that could be handled by a service assistant or a customer service representative.

Our firm has six advisors and a team of 9 full-time and 2 part-time people. Each advisor has four backup people, and that's a pretty good ratio. I think you want at least a two-to-one ratio, two assistants per advisor in the firm. So a firm with two advisors should have at least four staff people backing them up. If you get lower than this in today's economy, when investment firms and insurance companies push more and more paperwork out to the financial firm that they used to do for their advisors, it is going to be very hard for that broker to handle your account.

5. Community Recognition

The broker or advisor you choose should have a recognized name in the community. Let's think about a company like Disney. In Orlando, if somebody even writes the word *Disney* on a sign, Disney comes after them to take that word down. Disney makes sure that if it has the legal right to force the issue, it will do it simply because it wants to protect its reputation, a reputation second to none.

Other companies such as McDonalds and Coca Cola that have a very high level of service and brand recognition will do almost anything to protect that brand. They will decide not to take certain customers because they worry that those customers might be the complaining type, and the companies want to protect their reputation and their brand.

The same goes for financial advisors. Financial advisors who have a recognized name in a community will be very careful to bend over backward to do the right thing because they have spent years building their strong reputations and don't want to do anything to tarnish them. Choose an advisor who has a well-recognized name in the community.

6. Author = Authority

It is important that your advisor be an author. Has yours written articles? Has yours authored books? Does he have any kind of ownership of publications out there, including a website? Is the website part of a big firm like Merrill Lynch or Ameriprise, or is it independent?

Independent advisors will tend to have their own websites, not websites that are linked to big brokerage houses. It's helpful to know that your advisor has the expertise and the independence to write about subjects that are relevant to you.

7. Media Presence

This goes along with "Author"—find an advisor who has a media presence, someone the media trusts for knowledge and advice. TV and radio stations typically have certain people they go to in the community who are able to speak on a number of different subjects. Has your advisor been on TV or the radio in the role of a local expert? This can be a good indication of a good reputation.

8. A Good Business Person

Does your advisor know how to run a business? This goes back to the difference between an independent advisor and one who is just an employee of the firm. How somebody can handle millions of dollars of other people's money and have no clue how to run a business is beyond me. It's also beyond me that somebody would choose to work with an advisor who has no employees, who has no banking relationship or even a business checkbook, and who does not spend his or her own money on marketing and reputation. This is inconceivable to me.

Find an advisor who is independent and also understands the ins and outs of running a business, including hiring and firing employees, supervising customer service staff, and delegating issues as they come up instead of doing absolutely everything themselves.

9. Giving to the Community

Last but not least, find an advisor who gives back to his or her community. Someone willing to put money back into the community organically, not just for the sake of publicity such as sponsoring charity auctions so that an advisor can be seen with a prominent group. I'm talking about someone who is genuinely interested in supporting their community and will display a presence to those in need.

Keep these nine considerations in mind when you are in the process of choosing a financial advisor. Also try to make an individual list of your own values to expand upon the ones I have offered above. After all, this is about you and no one can protect you better then yourself.

Start with my list and begin to narrow down the advisors in your community; it is very possible that in an area like Connecticut, my state which has thousands of licensed financial advisors, you may come up with only 20 to choose from. But then you can begin to interview them, talking and listening, and end up with the one who is the best fit for you.